www.finishinglinepress.com

AYITI

Daniel Wolff

Finishing Line Press
Georgetown, Kentucky

AYITI

ACKNOWLEDGMENTS

"Some time in the night," "The National Palace" and "Our job is to intervene"
appeared in *Sub-Tropics*.
"The resurrection of hunger;" "The Road to Jacmel;" "The way the river
honors;" Kreyol;" and "Now…" appeared in *TLR*.
"Caribbean;" "The illusion of Haiti;" "Sightseeing;" "Look past the people;"
and "Backtrack" appeared in *Raritan Review*.
Thanks to all.

Publisher: Leah Maines

Editor: Christen Kincaid

Cover Art: Public Domain

Cover Design: Patricia Curtan

Printed in the USA on acid-free paper.
Order online: www.finishinglinepress.com
            also available on amazon.com

Author inquiries and mail orders:
Finishing Line Press
P. O. Box 1626
Georgetown, Kentucky 40324
U. S. A.

Table of Contents

"Haiti's major economic resources are the abundance of unskilled and semi-skilled labor and a sophisticated and dynamic private sector."
—U.S. Commerce Department, 1984

Human beings suffer
                    stubbornly wounded
and there are protests and weeping
                    everywhere:
—*Ode to Frederico Garcia Lorca*, Pablo Neruda, 1935

"No, I don't despair. I don't believe in despair, but our problems won't be solved by the Marines."
—*The Comedians*, Graham Greene, 1966

"I say: Disobey the rules. Ask for more. Leave your wretchedness behind. Organize with your brothers and sisters. Never accept the hand of fate. Keep hope alive."
—Jean-Bertrand Aristide, 1990

In anticipation of travel,
you watch your children
splash watercolor

on white paper,
try to remember
— in anticipation of travel—

what you will leave.

CARIBBEAN

The dark mountains seem to float on the light blue sea.

They don't.

They're attached to and the product of unseen pressure: the colliding forces of the North, South, and Central American tectonic plates. This pressure has helped produce some seven hundred islands scattered in a series of arcs between Florida and Venezuela.

This one – with its thick highlands feeding muddy rivers that end at tropical beaches—stayed nameless for millions of years. Then the Taíno and the Carib Indians arrived and, for three centuries, called it Ayiti: Land of Mountains.

In 1492 after his ship sank nearby, Christopher Columbus came ashore and established the first European settlement in the New World. The Spanish cleared land and built sugar plantations. For the next two centuries, the island was called Hispaniola: Little Spain.

In the 1600's, the French took control of the island's western third. They imported African slaves, exported coffee and sugar, and created the richest colony in the world: Saint-Domingue.

In 1791, there was an uprising. It's said to have begun with a ceremony honoring a new religion that combined African, European, and native Caribbean beliefs: a system called Vodou. After more than a dozen years, the slaves defeated Napoleon's armies and named their republic Haiti: the Caribbean's first independent nation.

It wasn't. It couldn't be.

Like the surrounding islands, like South America, Haiti remained attached to and the product of unseen pressure. Through the nineteenth century, a series of presidents, emperors, and kings oversaw a subsistence economy, as the new nation tried to pay off the debt France had imposed on it in return for recognizing the sovereign republic. By the twentieth century, the island had become a tourist destination, falling under what's been called the "colossal shadow" of the United States.

At the start of World War I, U.S. Marines landed and stayed for almost twenty years. They established an elite, light-skinned ruling class. François Duvalier was elected head of state in 1957 and soon declared himself President for Life. Fourteen years later, when Papa Doc died, the title passed to his son. Fifteen years after that, protests drove Baby Doc from the island. The U.S.-backed Haitian military took control, promising fair and open elections.

Four years later, the overwhelming majority of Haitians chose as president a former Catholic priest, community organizer, and anti-Duvalierist, Jean-Bertrand Aristide. "We must end this regime," Aristide declared, "where the donkeys do all the work and horses prance in the sunshine." He proposed a national literacy program, a higher minimum wage, and a redistribution of land. The military rejected the election and attempted to re-seize power, but President Aristede was inaugurated in February, 1991.

Six months later, he delivered a speech calling on the elite – a half-dozen families—to pay the back taxes they owed. "You who have money…That money in your possession, it is not really yours. You earned it in thievery... under an evil regime, an evil system…" A few days later, there was a military coup.

Aristide fled to Venezuela, and over a thousand of his supporters were killed. During the next three years, another five thousand were murdered, their bodies often displayed on the street as a warning. Some forty thousand tried to leave the island, many by open boat, many aimed at the coast of Florida.

In September, 1994, the U.S. decided to return Aristide to power. Twenty thousand troops landed at the Port-au-Prince airport, threw down sand bags, aimed their rifles – and found no resistance. Most Haitians greeted them with cheers, while sullen police and army officers handed over their weapons.

Under pressure to negotiate his return, President Aristide had signed an agreement with American and European representatives to back-off raising the minimum wage, to privatize state-owned businesses, and to encourage multi-national corporate development. Haitians described him as coming back *de pye nan youn gren soulye*: both feet in a single shoe.

He delivered his return speech from behind a bullet-proof bubble in front of the National Palace. "No to violence!" he declared. "No to vengeance! Yes to reconciliation!" Then he released a white dove: the Catholic symbol of the Holy Spirit and the *Vodou* symbol of sacrifice.

That was three weeks ago.

The illusion of Haiti
is the illusion
of dark mountains
that can be pried off a blue sea.
As if a stamp underneath
        read, "PROPERTY OF."

Look from above
at what relief
buys: dust slopes, sludge rivers,
piles of debris
that turn out to be
shelters.

Now, step into the heat.
Take a quick breath.
Is the taste of death
(sweet)
another illusion,
a trick?

Voodoo economics
is a term coined by a nation
rich enough for its citizens to say,
"You can only keep
what you give away."
The opposite of illusion is sleep.

SIGHTSEEING

An eight-year-old taps on the car window. His black skin has gone white at the corners of his mouth. "One dollar. Just one dollar."

You've been trained to smile and say no.

And if he won't go away? You know how to make him disappear: beyond his face are other faces.

And beyond them? Billboards selling beer.

If we saw and heard, that's all we'd do. The news would never change:

"Today is Tuesday: people who don't have enough to eat are asking people with more than enough to share.... Today is Wednesday: people who don't have enough to eat.... Today is Thursday: ...."

We come for the sights, taught not to see.

Look past the people.
You're driving
towards a mountain—a kind of steeple—
but keep arriving
at dust.
The trees have all been lost to charcoal.
You must
not turn back. You must drive past the beautiful
straight-backed woman, past her baby,
past the man's arms slashed across
his strong chest. Yes, the topsoil's gone, and maybe
the road's washed
out. But nothing erases desire.
You're driving towards fire.

BACKTRACK

First was the airport: like an army base, an army base in the American South, with blocks of green camouflage tents and mustard-brown jeeps, troops with silver weapons, radar spinning in the tropical sky.

It's being called an intervention, not an invasion. Or as some say, an inter-vasion. Its official goal is to provide temporary support for the return of democracy.

An historic moment. Not only because it's never happened before, but because it's happened again and again: historic return/the return of history. How long will the U.S. occupy this time? What is it whispering in the president's ear? How much will the island give up in order to stay independent? Variations on these questions are older than the republic. State Department attachés chopper into the guarded airport like the ghosts of Napoleon's commanders.

After the airport, there was the bay. Signs along its beaches said, in English: "DANGER: WATER TURNS BACK ON ITSELF..."

After the beaches, in an empty field, an old wrought iron scale. It stood as high as a man standing on top of a man. It had a claw to weigh how much sugarcane had been cut, how much profit would be made. It was rusted solid.

After the airport, the beaches, the iron scale, downtown Port-au-Prince is alive with people. They press against each other, everybody busy. Markets are open with piles of goods. Workers are re-lettering signs; masons re-build walls; painters freshen pink houses.

The white dome of the National Palace, built by the occupying Marines in 1920, looks like a slightly-off copy of the U.S. White House—which looks like a slightly-off copy of an 18th century French baroque dome – which looks like a slightly-off copy of a Greek temple. Three weeks after his return, the President is still inside, has yet to leave this building.

In a narrow alley near the Palace, you catch a glimpse of a child's body tip-toeing over a sewage-filled ditch. Is this your job: to take what you feel for your family and transpose it here? Do we call that journalism? Or poetry? Or tourism? And when does it become an occupation?

You drive past Port-au-Prince, up into the hills, to a wealthy area called Pétionville. Its hotels—the blue eyes of its swimming pools—look west past Cuba to Miami. What happens down in the city amounts to a low-level distraction.

They say that after twenty-seven years in prison, when Nelson Mandela was released, he built a room to the exact dimensions of his former cell. Not to re-live the suffering, he explained, but to be able to find the bathroom at night.

Some time in the night,
　　　　as the bougainvillea creeps a finger
　　　　higher on the stone wall,
the barking of the skinny dog changes.

The barking of the skinny dog
　　　　grows rougher and numerous:
　　　　many dogs. "Lavalas!" they bark.
Except it's not a bark; it's a chant.

Up the dark street they come:
　　　　"Lavalas! Lavalas!"
　　　　Hundreds of bare feet
climb out of the mud and up the hill.

At the doors of the rich,
　　　　they chant "Lavalas!"
　　　　It means a flooding or
overturning, as strong as any avalanche.

To which the rich
　　　　make no reply.
　　　　But a rooster answers,
"Aristide!"

A rooster crows in the dark:
　　　　a three-note call,
　　　　"Ar-is-tide."
The name of the priest turned savior.

"Lavalas!" the dogs all bark.
　　　　"Aristide!" the rooster answers.
　　　　As if it was already dawn,
as if the dark was gone for good.

A tourist sleeps in a tourist hotel,
        hears the noise,
        and to prove it's a dream,
wakes and walks to the window.

Lights lie strewn like trash
        on the city.
        Off in the distance,
the dark of the sea.

It isn't a dream. It isn't a dream.
        The tourist leans out
        to spot the mob,
its torches and clubs and crippled hands.

There isn't a mob;
        it isn't a dream.
        A rooster crows at a low moon;
a dog keeps barking.

THE NATIONAL PALACE

"When I was elected president, it wasn't a strictly political affair; it wasn't the election of a politician, of a conventional political party. No, it was an expression of a broad popular movement, of the mobilization of the people as a whole. For the first time, the National Palace became a place not just for professional politicians but for the people themselves."

-Jean-Bertrand Aristide, 2006

The security guards at the National Palace take our American drivers' licenses – laminated plastic – and exchange them for visitors' passes—worn paper. Then they show us through a metal detector. It's like a big modern scale: it weighs what we carry. While they check our credentials, we wait in a dirty white room lined with tiles.

After we've been okayed, an escort leads us around the side of the building to a set of monumental stairs. Across the green lawn, crowds have massed by the gates. They stare at us like we're somebody. And we're somebody because we're this side of the gates. We climb the stairs to the official entrance.

Inside, the wall-to-wall carpet is worn. Old chandeliers dangle from high ceilings. Along the wall, only four of ten marble sconces are left; the rest, we're told, were taken by the previous military government.

A set of double doors leads to a small balcony. If you stepped out, you'd be overlooking the green lawn and the gates and the crowds, who would probably cheer simply because you stepped out. Beyond them is the marketplace and the traffic, beyond that the airport with its base camp and the beaches, beyond that the Caribbean. If you were somebody, you'd wave to the crowds below. If this were your history.

While we wait, a helicopter lands on the lawn. The grass is blown in little green waves as officials disembark. They look American: men and women in suits with briefcases. They keep their heads down, below the blades. An escort of Marines hurries to greet them, and the officials clap the Marines on the shoulders, then dash towards the Palace.

We watch them the way the people at the gates watched us. Who are they? Why do they deserve this treatment? How will they change our lives?

A red-headed man comes in and begins to chat. He's wearing a heavy silver college ring – Princeton – and a tiny pink earpiece that whispers now and then. He talks about Aristide's first trip outside the palace, only a few hours ago. After the President gave a brief speech, he shook off his security guard and walked into the crowd, talking to people, touching them. They went wild. "A politician," the red-headed man explains, making it both compliment and criticism.

Moments later, we meet the President. He's small, unpresumptuous, a little wall-eyed. He seems delighted to be here – to be back in Haiti, to be in the palace. As he greets each person in the large circle of visitors, he's almost laughing out loud. It's like he's being carried on our shoulders, taken up.

He leads us back to his office. There's very little furniture. He points to the almost bare desk: "This is where I work." He shows us a back room with a pull-out couch and, past that, in the bathroom, three cushions stacked against the wall. "The First Bed," he calls it, smiling at the joke: the might of the American military airlifts him back into power so he can sleep on the floor. "Of course," he adds, "compared to most Haitians, this is paradise."

He speaks with careful modesty, like a priest. Aristede was expelled from his Salesian order six years ago. The reason given was "glorification of class struggle, in direct opposition to the teachings of the Church" and "using religion to incite hatred and violence." Technically, though, he stayed a priest till this month. And he still acts like he's a servant, doing the will of the people now, rather than—or as well as—God's.

If it's an act, it's a convincing one. Joyous, humble, enthusiastic, he talks with us till the red-headed man comes and whispers in his ear. Then the President bows out, apologizing. He has, he says, "official business."

We're led back through security, where they return our laminated licenses. We walk down the national drive to the national gates, where we stop to talk with the American guards. Outside, the crowd is mostly cripples and beggars.

"Our job is to intervene.
I mean, we already kicked butt.
Our orders are to stand between:
to supervise
the transfer of power
from the bad guys
to … whomever.
I was never
trained for this: eight hours
of guard duty
outside an empty jail.
Now and then, the wail
of big American cars
but mostly kids wanting candy bars.
Then what?
In a month or three, democracy."

The resurrection of hunger is courage:
        after the woman is buried
        —after we've studied the stains on her sheet –
        out of the dust, she'll rise, dazed.

        The crowd around her is the crowd around
        the National Palace – pushing against an iron fence
        where bored GI's in green flak jackets
        flash their silver guns.

        They think they protect the people's courage:
        a skinny little wall-eyed man
        with a bald spot on the top of his head.
        Like a tonsure. Like a monk.

                "Here's a riddle," his smile says:
                What turns the blades of the helicopter
                that churns the grass in front of the palace
                yet forces the people washed by that wind
                to bathe in an open sewer?

        The red-haired man with the heavy ring
        is sure he knows the answer.
        He's never been buried; he thinks he's alive.
        His job is to fax a condensed report
        and then rise behind it, north.

        If the riddle's answer is outside the gate
        —where legs can barely brace a body,
        where skin has begun to shred,
        where hunger beats like the biggest drum –
        then what are the guns guarding?

        Deep in the white of the National Palace,
        a little man sleeps on the floor, on a pallet,
        from which he cannot rise.
        The resurrection of courage is hunger.

THE ROAD TO JACMEL

The road to Jacmel is through the mountains. It cuts back and forth in an upward swirl like it's trying to get you over the top in one long, connected peel. It's built on some kind of oceanic limestone, and progress is measured by a series of look-backs. Behind you, against the green of vegetation, you can see the white of the rock. It marks where you've been, how far you've come.

The big city of traffic and stacked buildings is soon left behind. Here, there's the emptiness of mountains: an occasional tin roof on a steep slope among big-leafed sugar cane. Each house stands separately, a small rectangle of sheet-metal opened by the smaller rectangle of a door through which you can see blue sky.

Children in ripped t-shirts play by the road. One group beats sticks against a banana tree: some kind of game? Behind them, a great valley falls away. Above them, a bird of prey swoops and rises, looking for food. If it's a vulture, it's searching for the dead; if it's a hawk, the living.

At the crossroads, where the main route meets local trails, there's a market. Instead of the big city's constant cry, this is a weekly event. Women come down with green bananas, breadfruit, plastic bags of charcoal. They arrange their small displays on the curb and wait. It's still commerce, still the marketplace, but it seems more proportionate somehow. The sellers exchange their goods for paper money, *gourdes*, worn and stained with dirt. When the product's gone – or the day ends—the women climb back into the hills.

Is this how the world once worked? Hunger close, the sky enormous, home staked to the side of a slope, help and hurt local?

On the other side of the mountains, the road comes down in the same swirl. It ends in Jacmel, a town of balconies and broad streets and vistas over a white-blue sea. For all its pastel beauty and wind-blown quiet, Jacmel feels empty—as still as the future. You get here by looking back.

The way the river honors the dead
is to blush pink, then rush past.
The way the river forgets the machete
is to polish the bone white.

The river deposits the dead at the sea,
where they're not dead, but a tincture of red
that mixes in a larger body.
There, they end up saved. Or safe.

Where it begins is the marketplace:
piles of plastic propped in the mud,
second-hand shirts ironed and folded,
food stamped RELIEF.

Behind each careful display, a body
nods near sleep, jerks awake,
eyes the stream of passing cars,
brushes away flies.

If each seller declares a life,
each buyer shares the same.
So begins the long exchange
that ends at the river that ends at the sea.

KREYOL

The switch-backs up the mountains are called *karate* because they cut back and forth like the hands of a karate master.

Governmental attachés are called *samsonites*: for their luggage.

Matthew 15:27: "Yet the dogs eat of the crumbs which fall from their masters' table." President Aristide: "Haitians have always had to eat the crumbs that fall from the table. One day we will all sit around the table and share the cake."

A general who seized power during the last military coup announced, at the time, that it was no more likely for Aristide to return than for an egg to be put back in a chicken. In the National Palace, one of the President's aides proudly displays a political button showing a finger reinserting an egg.

The local buses, known as tap-taps, are covered with color: abstract designs, portraits, lettering. Loaded with people, they bounce along in stop-and-go traffic, as if paintings could carry passengers.

In the days after Arisitide's return, people decorated everything: rocks, trees, the sides of buildings. In Carrefour, a residential section outside Port-au-Prince, murals, known as *foto*—news photographs— change daily. One of the repeating characters is a rooster, the symbol of the Lavalas Party, with the bald head, wall eyes, and glasses of *Titid*, President Aristide.

Already in the stalls of the big markets, you can buy paintings of Marine choppers hovering over the Presidential Palace like swarms of green bugs. Stacked next to these are images that go back through Haitian history (or is it forward?):

• The occupation of the U.S. Marines in 1915. Distinguished from the current occupation only by the style of the uniform.

• The revolutionary hero, Henri Christophe, sitting at his presidential desk (like Aristide's desk), pointing a gun at his heart. In October, 1820, having gone from national hero to autocratic ruler, he killed himself with a silver bullet.

• Monsters lurking in green landscapes. These are boogiemen, the *Ton-ton Macoute*, who gave their name to the Duvaliers' private security force, now supposedly disbanded. In Haitian bedtime stories they kidnap and eat children.

The headline in a city newspaper—**POVERTY IN CAP HAÏTIEN ON RISE**—has the factual ring of a field guide. As if truth was a type of tree you could identify and measure.

In Latin, the big old trees are *Ceiba pentandra*. Common English name: the cotton or silk cotton tree, usually found near water. In Kreyol, it's *mapou*: a sacred tree that connects earth to sky. It has smooth muscular bark that seems to curve in on itself and long, snake-like roots. It's known to open at night like a door and reveal the spirits within. Sometimes it gets up and walks.

Now Now   Now   Now   Now.
In the green room, the *poto mitan*:
a pillar connecting ground to sky.
Where the snake would curl
if the snake should come.
The ceiling strung with printed portraits
of presidents past and present:
qui sont le même homme.

        This is not our language;
        this is not our home.
        What we know here
        is unknown.

Against green walls, dark bodies,
all of them dressed in white.
From the great-grandmother in a bright scarf
—her mouth bunched like a used purse—
to the teenage boy, gold-chained,
his muscles smoothed
with a charcoal thumb.
Witnesses stunned into life.

        What right have we to be here?
        Strangers on the outside;
        strangers on the inside.
        The skin of our wealth is white.

Two hundred bodies stuffed in a room:
the windows shuttered, the air wet,
the dirt packed down on the floor.
The only route out is the *poto mitan*,
which is not a route but a tree without limbs.
Then the drums begin to beat the light,
slowly turning it white-washed white,
till it dances beneath the shadows.

This is a place called Cité Soleil:
city of sun, of concrete and sweat,
city of pepper and cardboard distilled,
city of spit and *kleren*.

A chant starts up: almost words.
Words are feet with rounded heels.
They kick at the dirt, and clouds appear,
which coat the wet skin grey.
As the chanting rises, the shuttered room
picks the body of a thin-boned woman,
who moves with the others but can't stop moving,
like a bus climbing over mountains.

Where will she sleep?
What will she eat?
Twelve cents a day
selling smoke on the street.

Squeezed like a pit by the heat and drums,
unable to stand, unable to stop,
she spins and spins and spins against
the bodies that form a living wall,
that catch her weight before it can fall
but refuse to take her in, until –
spine rigid, muscles spent –
she pops from this world to the next.

Now it's done.   Now.
One hand limp in the settling dust.
Her white-washed eyes stare straight up
at the faces staring down.

Wrap her flesh in a fresh white sheet.
Stuff her nose and ears with cotton.
The ring of the drum strops the shovel
till it's nearly as sharp
as a blade.
Scrape a ditch in the dry dirt floor.
Lower her down with care.
Now spray her face with a mouthful of water.

> If this is the city of sun (it is),
> then the sun's gone dark, the night's opened up,
> and the earth is a distant, cooling rock—
> a spark in unlivable space.

The chant of the feet has never stopped.
Now a thin-shanked goat gets led to the center.
How could we know the inside of its throat
would be pink as bougainvillea?
Its almond eyes, upside-down,
blink at the empty ceiling.
Slowly the pink drips on her sheets,
turning black as a map of the city.

> Does she die for us?
> Are we white with her death?
> Is there room for breath
> between these beats?

The *houngan*/priest lets those who dare
jump across her unfilled grave,
then lifts her up—still bagged in her sheet—
and sets her on her feet.
Is she the one who enters, defiant,
then sags in a circle of white-palmed hands,
who's lost control but carefully steps
past the sack with almond eyes?

She opens her own and gapes at us.
Where is she now? What have we done?
Does she think she's been here all along?
Do we think we've been here with her?

In a green room, in a city of sun,
the world doesn't end at the tiny door
but opens onto an alley ripe
with hunger and shit, fruit and skin.
What wisdom has gathered across the years
settles from cloud back into dirt.
It stinks. It stinks of death and decay
and the breath that believes in   Now.

You dream you can always fly back home.
You dream you can pass through a modern building
—white concrete with rust-red shutters—

and a man in a suit will stamp your papers,
and you'll rise in a body that, maybe,
you dream. You can always fly back home.

But in this dream, you never do.

DANIEL WOLFF has published three collections of poetry, including *The Names of Birds* (Four Way Books). His poems have appeared in *The American Poetry Review, The Paris Review, Grand Street,* and the New York subway (illegally). He's also written poetry for collaborative projects with sculptors Robert Taplin and Harry Roseman, choreographer Marta Renzi, and songwriters Steve Elson and David Pulkingham, among others. Wolff has been nominated for a Grammy and written a number of non-fiction books. His latest, *Grown-Up Anger: The Connected Mysteries of Bob Dylan, Woody Guthrie and the Calumet Massacre of 1913* was a Michigan Notable Book; *The New York Times* called it "an elegantly written and insightful cultural history." He's produced documentary films with director Jonathan Demme, including *The Agronomist,* a study of Haitian journalist Jean Dominique, and contributed text to a number of photography books by Ernest Withers, Danny Lyon, and Eric Meola.

www.ingramcontent.com/pod-product-compliance
Lightning Source LLC
LaVergne TN
LVHW021123080426
835510LV00021B/3301